The Growth of Child Art

R. R. Tomlinson
O.B.E., R.B.A., A.R.C.A., P.R.D.S.

John FitzMaurice Mills
R.D.S., F.R.S.A.I., F.R.S.A.

The growth of child art

 UNIVERSITY OF LONDON PRESS LTD

UNIVERSITY OF LONDON PRESS LTD SAINT PAULS HOUSE WARWICK LANE LONDON EC4

Designed by Mary Fry

Text copyright © 1966 R. R. Tomlinson and John FitzMaurice Mills
Pictures copyright © 1966 *The Sunday Mirror*
Printed and bound by Hazell Watson & Viney Ltd Aylesbury Bucks

Contents

List of Plates

The History of the Teaching of Child Art

One hundred and fifty years ago the far-seeing Swiss educationalist, Pestalozzi (1746–1827), wrote, 'Understanding is only possible by that spontaneous perception which is the result of observation.' The moment of the awakening of the artist in a child can mark the way towards the true growth to an adult mind. It is a time of wonderful expectation as the great door of experience begins slowly to open, exposing to the child the endless vistas to follow. Today the art room in the school has moved up the ladder of importance. There the child can, with hands and materials, seek to develop ideas which pour out of the young mind, ideas that are sincere, fresh and untroubled. The art teacher holds something very precious in his hands, something which can so easily and quickly become dulled, can retire into itself frightened, or, perhaps worst of all, can turn into a slavish, easily satisfied desire to copy. The teacher must first of all encourage, and secondly, guide.

Philosophers as far back as Aristotle and Plato realized the need and the importance of training the hand as a means of developing the mind. Plato also recognized the need for aesthetics in education. The teachings and writings of these two great men dominated the intellectual world for hundreds of years until, towards the end of the Middle Ages, their views were supported by other great philosophers like François Rabelais (1490–1553). This writer was a great humanist and in his enthusiasm for his subject he often aroused the envy and jealousy of his fellows. A little later came Johann Comenius (1592–1671), the Czech educational reformer. He again was to stress the value of pictorial representations in fixing ideas on the memory. In the seventeenth century, John Locke, the English philosopher, claimed that the source of all knowledge is experience and that there is nothing in the intellect which is not already in the senses. Locke, by advocating the training of the senses, inspired the French philosopher Jean Jacques Rousseau (1712–1778), who developed the theory that instruction should proceed by an appeal to the child's curiosity, by stimulating his intelligence rather than by imposing cut and dried notions upon it.

From the work of Pestalozzi and the German educational reformers, Johann Herbart (1776–1841) and Friedrich Froebel (1782–1852), the Kindergarten system as we know it today began. The underlying principle of Froebel's teaching is that great stress should be laid on the value of giving freedom to the natural creativeness of the child mind.

Webster's dictionary defines imagination in several ways, which include this: 'The act, process, or power of imagining; formation of mental images of objects not present to the senses, especially of those never perceived in their entirety; hence, mental synthesis of new ideas from elements experienced separately.'

It was Trevisa in 1398 who first designated imagination as the faculty whereby 'the soul beholdeth the likeness of things that be absent'.

Again Webster concedes that this meaning still occurs in psychology under the name *reproductive imagination*. The broader meaning, already developed in Chaucer, starts with the notion of mental imaging of things suggested but not previously experienced, and thence expands to fantastic representation, or fancy, and later to the idea of mental creation and poetic idealization. Perhaps in that last word, the early poet starts to sum up the meaning of an education in art. It is the first turning away from purely physical experience to mental, a subliminal climb towards beauty and appreciation (translated as love), and away from the gross, the ugly, the discordant.

The vital link in the writings of all these great thinkers is the value of development through sense perception as well as through formal, academic mental training. They maintain that the training of hand and eye is as important as study of the classics, and that the essential thing is the development of skill and intelligence. Like many other new ideas, the theories of these men took a long time to seep through bureaucratic walls which are, unfortunately, sometimes the dam holding back the flow of new ideas in education. Ultimately, however, those in authority, here and abroad, did realize the necessity for change. Germany and Switzerland were the first to act, and in 1835 the British Government appointed a Select Committee to inquire into the best means of developing art appreciation among the people. The Committee later reported that it would be beneficial both to the artist and to the public to make art a part of general education in national schools. However, further years were to pass and no action was taken until after the Great Exhibition in 1851, when a renewed interest in design and craftsmanship was aroused. As a result, art teaching was at last introduced into the curriculum in state-aided schools.

How far, in the hundred odd years since this introduction, has art teaching, and, more important, have the results of art teaching progressed? In the middle of last century the first course of art training that was drawn up unfortunately had as its sole objective the development of skill with adult standards in view. Children were required to draw straight lines of varying lengths and directions, developed into cubes, pyramids and prisms; finally, curved lines were included as an introduction to the drawing of spheres, cylinders and cones. Black and white was the general limit of the materials supplied, and the whole essence of the drawing room (as it was then called) evaporated into a sterility which not only frustrated the child's creative desire, but turned the drawing room into a place of almost penal disenchantment. The drawing master himself was normally the least considered member of the staff. The generations who suffered under these first probes into art education must nearly have passed from us now: there can be few living who would be able to recall those early soul-destroying methods, but some grandparents may remember the freehand copy, the linear rendering of decorative features like the acanthus leaf on Greek or Roman capitals. In time, however, the syllabus began almost imperceptibly to broaden. What is known as mass drawing, done with a stump, light and shade, 'chiaroscuro', came into fashion. Later still came the 'back to nature' cult, which introduced the drawing of natural forms such as plants, flowers and fruit, and fashioned objects, flower-pots, jam-jars, boots, chairs—in fact, still life. An adequate art syllabus at that time was fully covered under the headings 'Object', 'Nature' and 'Ornament', without any mention of imagination. Ornament and patterns which were copied from classical or period examples were thrust at the young pupils, worn and chipped plaster casts from the Parthenon Frieze and other objects of classical veneration confronted them. During this long and sterile period, the ideas of the teacher were imposed upon the children. At that time, the second half of the nineteenth century and the early part of the twentieth, specialist teachers were recruited from the ranks of professional artists. It followed, therefore, that the development of technical skill, with preconceived adult standards in mind, was the principal aim. The professional artists, from whose ranks the teachers were drawn, would in the main be those most imbued with academic teachings, or those blindly following these obsolete precepts without any understanding of the child mind. How could they do other than to teach their own techniques and to insist on the application of rules formulated by adults for adults?

Frustration is one of the most dangerous influences in the development of the child's sensibility. Every teacher must, of course, be understanding and sympathetic and the art teacher most of all. His must be a selfless approach with an appreciation of the child's mind opening eagerly towards a warm sun of inspiration, a mind which will close up as readily as a flower when a passing cloud overshadows it. If it is not to be thwarted, freedom to express is essential in those vital, early years at school, for then creative power will either develop or atrophy. Just before the First World War, psychologists began to investigate the child's reaction to art and the stages of development through which children pass. They were assisted by teachers all over the country, and modern teachers owe a particular debt of gratitude to their research. More recently, Professor Stanley Hall, Sir Cyril Burt, Dr Ballard and Sir Herbert Read have illumined a clear path through the maze of uncertainties. The work of the psychologists and the writings of the ancient philosophers have inspired and guided pioneer teachers of art in both this and other countries. It is impossible to say which teacher of art to children first allowed them to create and express their own experience and conception in their own delightful and charming way, but mention should be made of the work of Professor Wesley Dow of America, Professor Cizek of Vienna, Mr Ablett, Founder of the Royal Drawing Society, and last, but certainly by no means least, Miss Marion Richardson for her devoted reforming work in London. But the pyramids, the cubes, the 'mass' drawing, the carefully arranged light and shade, the charcoal and the pencil as the sole art room tools disappeared very slowly. Even between the wars many schools were still in ignorance of the precious artistic talent wasting in their midst. To some extent the examiners were to blame. Time and time again, the young examinees found themselves faced with dull still-life objects, perhaps much more vividly and adequately described by the French term, *nature morte*. Imagination, it seemed, was not encouraged: was it something that

the teachers, the authorities, were afraid of, something that had to be kept firmly under control lest it should break out and reveal the inadequacy of the syllabus? But in this wilderness the oases grew in number and size. Isolated educationalists like John Howard Whitehouse, the founder of Bembridge School in the Isle of Wight, and others wrote theses on creative education, but through them all still echoed the words of the first philosophers of 'the hand and mind together'.

Examined, what does this principle produce? At work in the child it produces happiness and joy of creation. In the adult it can leave behind the inner satisfaction which comes from a healthy state and a sense of usefulness. During the last thirty years, however, there has been a remarkable advance in the teaching of art to children, who have been encouraged to draw, paint, model and carve in their own way, without any attempt to impose adult conceptions. All this, with the help, encouragement and love of devoted and understanding teachers, has had a most desirable and enlightening effect upon general education.

Here a short survey of craft education is appropriate. The word 'craft' comes from the Anglo-Saxon word *craeft* which, literally translated, means strength, power, skill, art. The last two qualities are those with which we are most concerned. In education the word 'craft' is understood to refer to a piece of handwork which has some claim to beauty. It is the result of a union of the craftsman's aesthetic feeling and his skill. The word used to describe industrial production has a different meaning, in that a product mechanically repeated has not the spontaneity or 'personality' of a handmade object. Craftsmanship is inseparably related to man's earliest work and development. The researches of the ethnographer, archaeologist and anthropologist have proved this. A knowledge of what was done in primitive times cannot fail to interest all who are concerned with the education of children. There is a sound basis of truth in the recapitulation theory; that is, that the development of the child follows a course rather like that of the race. The work of the teacher must first be a dedicated one, and it is essential for the teacher's mind to be as open and receptive as the mind of the child he is guiding, sensitive not only to the creative efforts of that child, but also to the tremors of fresh inspiration in the world of education around him, so that he is able to separate the grain from the chaff and bring that grain to fruition.

Works such as *Evolution in Art* by Dr A. C. Haddon, F.R.S. (Walter Scott, 1895), and *Decorative Patterns of the Ancient World* by Sir Flinders Petrie (British School of Archaeology in Egypt, 1930), can be studied with advantage, and with them the excellent guidebooks to the ethnographical sections in the British Museum. The graffiti of the early man in caves, the low-reliefs of the Egyptians, the present-day Bushman paintings, the more sophisticated of the *avant-garde* work today are all signposts on a long trail. They are all means of communication. In the earliest examples, primitive art speaks of the need for mere survival, a need perhaps influenced at times by magic and ritual. With the passing of time the communication becomes more subtle, marked by more intelligence and less instinct. But, most important of all, it is a means of communication which has a characteristic that is missing from every other kind, whether it is wireless, writing or any kind of signals: the communication of the visual is international. It knows no language barrier, and should know no barrier between one age group and another. A child working in a small village school in the depths of India can, on his paper, with brush and colour, portray something which can be understood by the child in Hong Kong, in the outback of Australia or the far north of Canada.

Craft teaching in schools has passed through many experimental stages and been known by many names. It has been termed 'manual training', 'hand and eye training', 'motor training', and, most recently, 'handwork', 'handicraft' and 'applied art'. Its chief claim to a place in the curriculum for many years was its value as a means of training the hand and eye. The teaching of art and craft in the past has tended to produce two kinds of people: first, the practical person with skill but without vision; secondly, the visionary without the opportunity or power to express his visions. Therefore, some understanding of the terms 'handicraft' and 'craft' as they are used today, and of our own purpose in teaching them, seems called for. There has not been this close and desirable association in the past between the teaching of art and craft, or the freedom of expression allowed in so-called 'handicraft departments', where the copying of set models still largely persists. Art and craft teachers are now beginning to collaborate and to encourage children to express their ideas in a wider range of materials, in their own way. Craft teachers have difficult problems to solve, for they have claims from those who would direct craft teaching towards technology and precision engineering; indeed, some plead the case for engineering and engineering draughtsmanship as an end in itself. Others believe that the sole purpose of craft teaching is to develop the child's creative powers and good taste. All these aspects have their place and claims in a liberal education, and this division of opinion is unfortunate. Both science and the arts should progress together if we are to live a full life. However, it is with the development of the child's creative ability and good taste that this book is most concerned.

In the art room today, what are the methods that are available to the child? Art teachers in some schools have to compete with a staggering variety of techniques, all of which they are expected to be able to practise and teach. Painting methods have fortunately overcome the restrictions imposed by the small black and white japanned water-colour box, with its little hard cakes of paint which have to be scrubbed vigorously with a brush for several minutes before they yield enough colour. In the art room there can be found large tins of powder colour, pots and tubes of rich poster colour, new types of colour cake which will dissolve rapidly. A more recent introduction is oil colour in an economic form, in big tins. Latest of all, synthetic resin colours in tubes and plastic jars can be used in every conceivable way, from most delicate tints of water colour to thick impasto and textured effects. They even allow the building up of collage, because the colours are adhesive.

No technical development in art education has done more to help the child express himself fully and freely than the introduction of powder colour and the consequent use of large sheets of paper. Previously, drawing books of about seven inches by five were in general use in maintained and state-aided schools. Their small sheets of paper gave no scope for freedom of movement or expression in either drawing or painting. Powder colour was first introduced in a wide range of tints in London schools in the early thirties, and was perfected with the co-operation of two of the principal colour manufacturers and the London Art Inspectorate. The replacing of the small water-colour box and hard colour cakes by powder colour, and latterly by readily soluble colour cakes, has also meant that larger brushes can be used in place of the small restricting pointed kind. This introduction of new materials has made it possible for the child to make broader, freer and more vital statements like those to be seen in schools today.

Printing processes will range from the humblest potato cuts in the lower classes of the primary school to lino cuts, wood, plaster and clay blocks, even to etching, engraving and silk screen printing.

The craft of printing itself is now being introduced into a great many schools which possess a small printing press and a limited range of type faces and wood capitals. The printing craft is closely associated with art history and the art course. A study of the work of primitive man has taught us that before writing as we know it today was invented, drawings of men, animals, objects and scenes were used for two purposes, and may be divided into two classes: pictographs, drawings used to convey information; and symbols, drawings used as marks of identity.

The first class, the pictograph, conveyed in no unmistakable way the thoughts of one man or tribe to another. The pictograph was eventually abandoned for the second class, the symbol. These drawings or symbols, besides developing into heraldry, one of the most beautiful types of decoration, progressed to one of the most interesting forms of writing of all time, the Egyptian hieroglyphic. Hieroglyphics are nothing more or less than drawings of people, animals, birds and so on, each drawing being a symbol which conveys a meaning. These symbols became simplified into letters. Letters were not invented by printers; they were copied and multiplied by them.

The letters we use today were first made by the scribe who was an artist craftsman. Calligraphy, the work of the scribe, is in fact a species of drawing. The relationship between the scribe, the artist and the printer has been maintained up to the present day: the artist designs the type and arranges and spaces it agreeably upon the page in fine relation to the illustration; the craftsman makes and sets up the type, and produces the printed page. The possession of a printing press in the art department enriches the art course considerably, for it provides design problems of the greatest value to the school as a whole, such as designing invitation cards, leaflets, posters and the school magazine. These can be carried out by arrangement of type alone, or of type in relation to potato cuts, lino cuts and simple wood cuts. When there are facilities for lithography and etching, as in the art departments of some of the new comprehensive schools, the combinations can be used most effectively.

When the printing course is associated with book binding and book production, the link between the art and craft course and general education is most valuable. For if book production with its literary implications is included in the syllabus, it can bridge the gap between different subjects, and connect the art and craft learned at school with everyday out-of-school life. Many reasons are advanced in favour of teaching printing and book production to children, but the fact that it fosters love for and interest in books—life-long friends—should be enough to assure it a place in the art and craft course.

Writing is every man's craft and yet it is the least considered and most neglected. Education authorities are now realizing this more and more clearly. Only recently the London County Council issued a pamphlet on handwriting, the main object of which is to draw attention to the neglect of this basic subject. The Royal Drawing Society, which conducts graded examinations in drawing and painting for children of all ages, because of the renewed interest, included handwriting as a subject in its series. Concern is felt not only by educational authorities, but by many others, lest children's handwriting should suffer large scale deterioration and descend into illegibility. A child's progress and power of expression are hindered by the inability to write clearly and with ease. The qualities considered essential to good writing are legibility, spacing, with fine arrangement on the page in mind, and a knowledge of the letter forms basic to the writing favoured by the individual or the school. The origin of writing has already been considered briefly in the paragraph on printing, but the history of the development of contemporary styles of lettering and writing will be helpful.

Writing can be traced back to the dawn of history. There is ample evidence that man tried to communicate his thoughts by this means throughout the ages. The development of the letters we use today is a fascinating story, and readers are referred to *A Handwriting Manual* by Alfred Fairbank (Faber & Faber, 1954) and *Writing and Illuminating and Lettering* by Edward Johnston (Pitman, 1906) for a full account.

The crafts of lettering in particular and of calligraphy in general are very closely associated with the art courses; letter shapes reached perfection in the carving on the Trajan Column and, based upon them, present-day styles, particularly those designed by Edward Johnston and Eric Gill, are most worthy of note. The term 'calligraphy' is used to denote fine penmanship, but because cursive writing is closely associated with the craft of calligraphy with its claims to beauty, the responsibility of the art teacher cannot devolve on to teachers of general subjects. The three styles in general use in schools are: italic, Marion Richardson, or round (Civil Service) hand. All these are legible, but the most elegant and lucid is the italic. This was evolved in Italy in the fifteenth century. It is the only style with an acknowledged beauty of form that has stood the test of time, to which reference can be made for a consistent standard. Originally written with an edged quill, it derives its beauty from the interplay of thick and thin strokes. Although the quill has long gone out of use, a generous variety of square-cut nibs suitable for italic writing is now on the market.

But it is when the teacher comes to traditional and newly discovered materials that the variety runs almost riot. The constant introduction of new materials, plastics, etc., adds to the infinite possibility for creative work. In these materials the young mind can see a vision of kaleidoscopic colour, composition and form. In the nursery school the young child will not have the muscular control to develop his vision, the co-ordination necessary between hand and eye and mind; but, given freedom of expression, he will feel the excitement when for the first time a large sheet of paper is spread in front of him, some brushes are laid out and large pots of colour opened. The young artist of five or six years old is searching to understand what everything is about. The whole of every day is taken up with discovery and, in the art room, it is discovered by experiment with paints and materials. The young mind sees everything simplified and the teacher who would focus a child's mind on details and insist on their reproduction is shutting the door against the child's own interpretation. The results of this kind of frustration are immeasurable. The child at this early age can have his attention and effort focused on only one thing at a time and can for brief periods show a power of concentration and single-mindedness that can be the envy of a mature artist. The young painter or craftsman will use his materials tentatively also to express a deep satisfaction. The colours he chooses are those that appeal to his emotion; the shapes that he starts from have appealed for the same reason. But care should be taken to avoid over-stimulating the young mind. The imagination may become so charged that it over-intensifies emotions and feelings. Again, extreme care is necessary with the verbal descriptions presented to a child. The teacher should make a serious study of the stages of development through which a child passes if he is not to find himself ill equipped for his task. He must not think in terms of ideas or pictures that will frighten a child. There should be no division between generations; we should all be able to enjoy that which gives pleasure to all ages. We should be able to appreciate work liked by those both behind and ahead of us. To the young child, a large lump of modelling clay is something which is challenging and not to be resisted. The big pots of mixed colour are as exciting as anything he has ever seen. They are not what the adult thinks of as a possible source of mess and untidiness, and any impression of this kind should be dispelled, even if it means that a great deal of clearing up has to be done after school hours. Teaching art can be a most rewarding experience to a teacher, and one which can give an almost unbelievable stimulus to his own growth and work. At the same time, the teacher should respect the works of his young charges just as much as if they were his own. Children may not always say very much, but they will certainly notice if at the end of the period their paintings are hastily gathered up, wet and dry together, and casually dumped because there is no room to store them. At the end of the year, Exhibition Day is one of the red letter days for the young pupil, whether he admits it or not, when he can come into the room or hall and find on show paintings and carvings that he himself has done in school.

A young painter of six or seven years old can portray with an almost overpowering truth the idea he is trying to express. These young artists are not fettered by fashion or by bigoted ideas. They are not afraid to show something of the way they see and feel, they are not afraid of bright colour and boldness, and in their simplicity they can achieve an incisive quality denied to many artists much older than themselves. Unfortunately, even today this creation, this grasping of the very tap-roots of sensitivity, can still be bruised by the fashion, the rat-race, the fears of the adult world when it is reached; but the art teachers, the psychologists, the philosophers who have laid the foundation for art teaching and art appreciation as it is now practised with young children in the large majority of schools and institutions, have put within the grasp of these coming generations tools and possibilities wholly denied to their fathers.

Exhibiting Child Art

Few things can be more stimulating and helpful to children than to see the work of others of their own age. Nothing quite equals the excitement of visiting a gallery to see their own work hung beside the best from all over the country and often from all over the world.

Today, many obstacles in the way of art education have been overcome. The art room, instead of being a boring place of little opportunity, is now complete and full, with the opportunity for the child to develop his own instinct and talent. Materials are available not only for painting but also for creating. Pots of bright colour, tubes of oil and water colour, chalks, pastels, many different papers, boards, canvas boards, provide the impetus for the child's imagination. The craft sections range from pottery to weaving, and basket-work to fabric printing and many others.

The importance of child art exhibitions and competitions cannot be over-estimated. Their influence on the work of the child can be immense. It was T. R. Ablett who was the first art teacher to recognize the importance of children's 'scribbles', and it was he who first had the courage to free the children in this country from the old copying method to the principle of self-expression. His pioneer work released children from the so-called 'freehand drawing', the official system of drawing for seventy years. This attractive name was a misapplication: it simply meant that the children were not allowed to use compasses, rulers or other instruments in their work. It was, in Ablett's own words, 'a dreary discipline of copying lines', the sole aim of which was to train the children into extreme accuracy of drawing. The system has now disappeared and the principles embodied in Ablett's original system of 'drawing from delight' have taken its place. Children from all over the world, literally millions, have taken Ablett's examinations, liberated from the hated 'freehand' system, and he may be justly called 'the children's friend'. He died in 1945 at the grand age of ninety-six. A fitting epitaph was written by his old pupil, who himself owed his success in life to drawing, Air Marshal Sir Roderic Hill, the man entrusted with the air defence of Great Britain during the last war, Equerry to King George VI, who, on his return to civilian life, became Rector of the Imperial College of Science and Technology and afterwards Vice-Chancellor of the University of London. Air Marshal Sir Roderic Hill wrote: 'The passing of Mr Ablett must have brought sorrow to thousands of people all over the world, especially to the children, many now grown up, for whom he cared and did so much. As one of those past children I should like to express my profound admiration of his work, which has not only brightened innumerable lives but has, in my belief, altered the whole outlook of two generations on the part that drawing can play in general education.' T. R. Ablett also founded the Drawing Society, now known as the Royal Drawing Society, which today does so much to guide child art in schools and also provides its own examinations in the many different subjects that come under the heading, Art Education. It was two years after the founding of the Royal Drawing Society that Mr Ablett held his first exhibition, indeed, the first exhibition of child art ever to be organized in Great Britain and possibly in the world. Up to that time few people had any idea that children could produce drawings and pictures worthy of consideration. The exhibition was literally an 'eye-opener' and people flocked to see it. Appreciation of the young people's efforts was shown by the President of the Society, Queen Victoria's artist daughter, Princess Louise, Duchess of Argyll, when in 1852 she purchased a picture called 'Babyland' by a girl of twelve, which contained a hundred and twelve figures in water colour, all in different dresses and attitudes, and presented it to Queen Victoria.

One of the main objects of the Royal Drawing Society is to discover talented children by means of its graded art examinations and exhibitions, to encourage them by awards and to help them in their careers by its advice. Many eminent artists living today owe their first recognition and encouragement to the Society. Air Marshal Sir Roderic Hill has already been mentioned. Others include Sir Gerald Kelly, Past President of the Royal Academy, who has said that his first success in life was when as a boy he had a picture hung in the 'Children's Royal Academy'. Another exhibitor was Robert Austin, R.A., a Past President of the Royal Water Colour Society; so was his fellow Academician, A. R. Thomson, R.A. Two others, at the head of their profession, are Edward Halliday, President of the Royal Society of British Artists, and Claude Rogers, President of the London Group. Another, whose passing during the war was a sad loss to the arts, was the brilliant Rex Whistler, whose delightful murals adorn the restaurant at the Tate Gallery. As a lieutenant in the Welsh Guards he was killed in 1944 at the age of thirty-nine, just after he had landed in France. He was one of the Society's students and some of his remarkable drawings from the age of five upwards are among the Society's treasured possessions, as well as his first oil painting when he became a student of the Slade School of Art at the University of London.

The formation of Ablett's Society in 1888 was the signal for a remarkable band of enthusiasts to range themselves behind him. They included not only artists and educationalists but leaders of progressive thought in many walks of life. Their names include not only the President, H.R.H. The Princess Louise, but also the then President of the Royal Academy, Lord Leighton; Sir James Linton, President of the Societies of Painters in Oil and of Painters in Water-Colour, who became Ablett's first Chairman of the Council; Holman Hunt, a member of the Pre-Raphaelite Brotherhood; Sir John Tenniel, the famous humorist of *Punch* and illustrator of Lewis Carroll's *Alice in Wonderland*; James Bryce, later Viscount Bryce, British Ambassador to the United States; W. E. H. Lecky, the historian; and later still, Viscount Burnham, originator of the Burnham Scale of teachers' salaries, Sir John Cockburn, and many other important figures.

The most generous of the many tributes that Ablett received came from Lord Baden-Powell. He admitted that without the splendid help of Mr Ablett he could never have succeeded as he had done and thanks were due to him and the Society for the great work they were doing. (For many years Ablett examined all work submitted for the Scout badge for drawing, which was called the 'artist's badge'.)

Shortly after Ablett founded the Royal Drawing Society in Great Britain, Professor Cizek, working independently on similar lines in Vienna, founded his famous Juvenile Art Class in 1897. For many years he had to fight against criticism and ridicule from the die-hards in education, as indeed Ablett did in this country.

Both these pioneer teachers believed that each child is a law unto himself and should be allowed to develop his own technique, that he cannot be subjected to a course of rigid technical training without stifling his creative power. During the past thirty or forty years, the shadows of the past have been gradually dissipated and teachers have seen not only the wisdom but the wonderful possibilities of this true freedom, particularly in art education. They have come to understand how, by rigid discipline in the past, untold talent, even perhaps genius, has been suffocated until it has died through the lack of imagination of those in authority.

Hundreds of British teachers visited Professor

Cizek's Juvenile Art Class in Vienna, but it was his Exhibitions of Children's Art held in London in 1934 and 1935 which first attracted the attention of educationalists in this country and gave an added impetus to changing methods and outlook.

These exhibitions, pioneer efforts as they were, prepared the ground for a change in the methods of teaching art to children. But still progress was slow, and it was not until the important Exhibition of Children's Drawings and Paintings at the County Hall, London, in 1938 that the majority of teachers were at last convinced that new methods were immediately desirable. The exhibition was organized and arranged by the London Art Inspectorate and showed the influence of the devoted work of Miss Marion Richardson.

Modern methods are the result of the cumulative researches and discovery of pioneer teachers and psychologists during the last hundred years, but it can be truly said that their acceptance by education authorities is largely due to her untiring work and to the work of those who came under her influence.

The most useful way to explain Miss Richardson's ideas is to quote her own words from the pamphlet issued for the opening of the exhibition by Sir Kenneth Clark. She said:

'Five years ago, we held an exhibition of children's drawings at County Hall. On that occasion the drawings came from fifty London schools and were, most of them, by very young children. The present exhibition is the result of an invitation to all London schools and the work chosen is mainly from the older pupils.

'There is a family likeness about the drawings in this exhibition, although they have been painted by at least 500 different children and come from a great many different schools. Every drawing, except those in Group Ten, is unmistakably a child's drawing and we accept this childlike quality as the sign of its sincerity. But many, many drawings sent in and yet unhung were also childlike. For what reason then were those before us chosen and others refused? The answer is that the final choice fell on those that were in some measure little works of art.

'In the face of so many glaring faults of drawing, some will find this bold statement merely bewildering, but the truth is that no work of art will ever be understood while looked at as though it were a photograph; and since it is impossible to look at these drawings in that way, let us—if we have not already done so—take the first step towards understanding art by recognizing it as the impression of an illumined state of mind and not an attempt to catch a likeness. Everything then depends upon an enlightened vision which is to the artist his idea. Everything? Yes, everything. Skill, the means of expression, can be found if only the idea is right.

'What is the nature of the artist's idea? It is always a visual idea, always to do with seeing, whether by the mind's eye or the physical eye. The artist discovers in the world around him (that is to say, in his raw material) relationships, order, harmony—just as the musician finds these things in the world of sound. This cannot be done by the conscious, scheming, planning mind. Art is not an effort of will but a gift of grace—to the child at least, the simplest and most natural thing in the world. Whenever people are sincere and free, art can spring up; the present exhibition is a witness to this fact. That is why the child's happiness or otherwise in the presence of the teacher is all important, and why the school of today is, or should be, the perfect setting for children's art. It is not too much to say that unless a relationship amounting to love exists between teacher and children, children's art, as we now understand it, is impossible.

'How does this love translate itself into action? For work such as we see here is not "free expression" as generally understood, which may be merely unconscious imitation, but a disciplined activity in which the teacher's own imaginative gifts play a very important part.

'There is no single answer to this question, the one which everyone asks. Each teacher finds his individual solution to the problem and those who can spare time to visit the schools will be struck by the variety and flexibility of modern methods. One essential is established. The good art teacher will always take his children and their drawings completely seriously. Perhaps this counts for more than anything else and is the means of inducing the children to demand the very best of themselves. They need, especially as they approach self-consciousness, the authority of a grown-up to convince them that their own art is worth while and to warn them against accepting the ready-made and second-hand which surrounds them on every side. This seriousness comes easily to the teacher as he realizes that his work with children may in the end provide for him a key to the understanding of art in its widest sense.

'It is to meet those doubts and difficulties that the present exhibition has been prepared. We feel that the time has come for showing what the big, as well as the little children, have achieved. The new method is still young. There has not yet been time for a child to pass right through school life since the first schools decided on a fundamental change of approach, but even so we have been able to show the development of a few children over a period of years and to devote most of the space in the exhibition to the work of senior, central and secondary schools.'

Exhibitions of child art have grown up in the last thirty years, and those today would hardly be recognized by the first exhibition held in London in 1889. It is difficult to express sufficient gratitude for the far-sighted patronage by the *Sunday Pictorial* (latterly the *Sunday Mirror*) for starting, since the last war, the National Exhibition of Children's Art. The jury for this is composed of practising artists, psychologists and art teachers, all of whom have that inherent love of child art and the wisdom to see its true value. In early autumn each year this exhibition takes its place on the list of national events, and in galleries in London and the principal cities can be seen the results of present-day work, and the remarkable advance made in art education can be appreciated. The teaching of child art has burst the bonds of obsolete and sterile methods. Imagination and creative power have here come into their own. This must surely pave the way for an enriching future not only for the individual artists and designers but for the rest of us around them. This enrichment, this release of talent is hard to measure immediately, and it will only be fully seen with the passing years. From the beginning, the National Exhibitions of Children's Art have been under the chairmanship of Sir Herbert Read, and the original panel of judges consisted of well-known critics and authorities on art teaching: with Sir Herbert Read were Philip James (Director of Art of the Arts Council of Great Britain), Mrs N. T. Lazenby (Member of the Society for Education in Art), Sir John Rothenstein (Director of the Tate Gallery), Professor Randolph Schwabe (Slade Professor of Fine Art, University of London), W. M. Whitehead (General Secretary of the National Society for Art Education) and R. R. Tomlinson (Senior Inspector of Art, London County Council).

In the foreword of the first catalogue for the exhibition of 1948, under the heading 'Art cannot be "tested"', Sir Herbert Read wrote: 'Most of the exhibitions of children's art held in this country have hitherto been highly specialized—that is to say, they have represented the work of a particular school or group of schools, or perhaps the results of a particular method of teaching. The National Exhibition of Children's Art is rather in the nature of an open academy; any school or individual within the limits of age laid down, is free to submit work and the only qualifications made in advance relate to the size and materials to be employed, and not to style or subject matter.

'I am speaking for myself and not necessarily for all my colleagues on the selection committee, but I would say that as we pass hundreds of paintings in review our attention is held by those which we find "expressive". Now this word "expressive" is like a red rag to some bulls in the educational field, so I must attempt to explain clearly what we mean by it. Education is impressive, repressive and expressive. We attempt to *impress* certain facts on the child's mind (and the result we call knowledge). We attempt to *repress* certain instincts in the child which are egotistical and anti-social, and we call the result manners or discipline. But we also (and this after all is the literal meaning of the word "education") try to bring out the native gifts or capacities of the child, and we can only do this by encouraging the child to *express* itself. There are various means of expression—verbal, vocal, musical, dramatic, choral, choreographic, graphic—and they are perhaps best regarded as different methods of *play*. In expressing themselves by such means children enjoy themselves and each other, loosen up and freely re-combine, and above all bring to the surface and harmlessly project those instincts which the impressive and repressive phases of education tend to frustrate. The degree of enjoyment expressed in such activities is the standard by which they can be judged. But the degree of enjoyment does depend, to some extent at any rate, on the degree of skill which the pupil has developed, and skill is merely good play—accurate, instinctive responses due either to native endowment or assiduous practice. It is not an imitative activity—the best cricketer is not the one who most successfully imitates Don Bradman, nor is the best painter the one who most successfully imitates the President of the Royal Academy. We become "good" at something by developing our own potentialities, and education is the art of discovering a child's particular gifts and giving these their best chance. The child is naturally creative; the child is a born artist. But the child is naturally shy of its fumbling efforts, and easily discouraged by impatient parents and unsympathetic teachers. If parents wish their children to develop their native gifts, they must give them the means—paper, crayons, paints, clays, etc.—and give without stint. And they must put up with a good deal of untidiness. A passion for tidiness is the beginning of philistinism. The right kind of tidiness will come with the growth of artistic consciousness. A child will soon learn the beauty of orderliness—but it must be discovered, it must be loved for its own sake. The other way leads to frustration, and frustration to aggression.

'The difficulty of preserving expressive freedom increases as the child grows; it is overwhelming by the time the examination stage is reached. Art dies in the dry atmosphere of intellectual tests. Nevertheless, the most surprising feature of the first exhibition is the relatively high quality of the art in the higher age groups. This may be pure chance, and is partially explained by the exceptionally high standard of work from one district—the city of Edinburgh. I suspect the presence in that city of a teacher or inspector who knows that art need not be sacrificed to the School Certificate, or to the myth of schoolboy manliness.

'The belief that art does not matter is betrayed in an almost universal poverty of materials. Paper for parcels is given priority over paper for pupils; schools can only beg, bargain and barter for what the grocer can spare from his sugar-bags. In all arts there is inspiration in the materials, but it is only an exceptional artist that is inspired by the mean rubbish offered to the average child in school. A wide reform is called for in this respect.'

The original and subsequent panels of judges consisted of prominent teachers, art organizers and art critics with some changes in their composition every year. The object of the sponsors of the exhibition was clearly expressed in the foreword of the 1948 catalogue by Sir Herbert Read which has just been quoted.

No exhibition had previously been organized in this country on a national scale and the response was most gratifying. The sponsors offered a £250 training award to be given to an exhibitor whose work was of outstanding merit in the upper age group, and further, many monetary awards to pupils in other age groups and to the schools concerned. These awards have been greatly appreciated and have helped several boys and girls to continue training both here and abroad.

The early exhibitions were confined to the graphic arts, painting and prints. This limitation was imposed because of the difficulties of packing and transport, not only to and from the schools and exhibition galleries, but also when the exhibition itself went on tour. So crafts were at first excluded. Eventually, however, in view of the close association between the arts and crafts and the solving of the difficulties of transport, the crafts were included.

Some children prefer to express their ideas in various materials. Since their inclusion in the exhibition, the crafts chosen have changed from year to year. Craft work such as pottery and weaving, fabric printing and puppetry, printing and book-binding take their turn, with rewarding results.

Perhaps the most attractive, even touching examples of highly imaginative toys and objects are made from stray pieces of junk collected by the children living in an unpromising environment.

Children are naturally imitative and are influenced by contemporary fashions and movements in painting, sculpture and craftwork. Consequently the vogue for abstract painting has been noticed and practised by them, sometimes with quite amazing and inspiring results. In sculpture, the most moving example in recent exhibitions is one entitled 'Fred' (Plate 102), made by a group of children from old tin cans, wire and bicycle pedals, picked up on rubbish dumps and on their wanderings.

Because of the numerous examples of sculpture submitted, sculpture, which is really a branch of so-called 'fine art', is included annually and is considered with painting for the Art Training Award.

Dr Wilhelm Viola, quoting the opinion of Franz Cizek, wrote in his book *Child Art*: 'It is a fact not to be denied, that many city children lose their creative ability in drawing and painting in the years of puberty. Might it not be an explanation that puberty, that period of struggle, so absorbs the whole of the adolescent being that nothing is left for creative activity?'

Although the difficulties experienced by the upper age group with the onset of puberty and concentration on examinations have resulted in a disappointing response, the signs of advance so evident in the younger age groups are appearing in the older ones. Teachers today do not agree that a lack of interest in creative work is inevitable at the age of thirteen or fourteen plus, and the results of the Art Training Awards each year have proved that it is not so generally. They do agree, however, that the problem needs urgent attention. With this in mind, each member of the panel of judges for the 1960 Exhibition wrote in the catalogue of that year their ideas for a solution or a means of carrying over creative activity through adolescence into adult life.

The Selection Committee for 1960 again included Sir Herbert Read as the Chairman, and E. M. O'Rourke Dickey, formerly Staff Inspector for Art for the Ministry of Education; Andrew Nairn, Superintendent of Art, Glasgow Education Committee; Eduardo Paolozzi, sculptor; Victor Pasmore, artist; R. R. Tomlinson, formerly Senior Inspector of Art, London County Council; and Gabriel White, Director of Art, the Arts Council of Great Britain.

It is felt that this problem is so important—since it concerns not only children of school age, teachers and parents, but the careers of school-leavers—that the opinions of this panel should be quoted in full.

Sir Herbert Read
'The Advisory Committee of the National Exhibition of Children's Art has, during its thirteen years' experience, become increasingly aware of one problem in the teaching of art to children. It is, indeed, a problem with which every art teacher is familiar. The profound change that each child undergoes at the onset of puberty has a devastating effect on its "will to art". I use this Germanic expression because it points to the subtle nature of the problem, which is a problem of consciousness and not a failure of skill or ability. We

say that the child "loses interest", and that expression again indicates that we are in the presence of a psychological problem.

'It was decided that this year, instead of the usual introduction to the catalogue of the exhibition, each member of the Advisory Committee should write some brief observations on this problem, and that I should co-ordinate and present them. I have limited my task to the arrangement of the observations in a more or less logical order. Mr Tomlinson, on the basis of his very wide experience, gives a general outline of the problem, then Mr Nairn makes the specific suggestion that during "this period of imaginative recession" the main emphasis in teaching should be on design and the crafts, with a gradual insistence on a higher degree of representational accuracy in painting. Mr White suggests that more harm than good may be done by forcing the child at this difficult stage, and that we must reconcile ourselves to a phase of dullness and effort while the latent forces prepare for the possibility of future achievement. Mr Dickey would rely on the sympathetic teacher to guide the pupil through this difficult period, but Mr Pasmore suggests that sympathy is not enough, nor is any negative reaction to the problem. A challenge to the adolescent must be made in terms of greater skill and higher mental development, and Mr Paolozzi suggests that this can be achieved by means of a spiritual activity in sympathy with the fast-moving cultural changes of an epoch.

'I myself agree with Pasmore and Paolozzi. The problem is a real challenge to the advocates of "the new art teaching", but it is not a problem that can be solved by an admission of defeat, nor by a retreat to the representational standards of academic art. It is true that the child of the age we are discussing needs the challenge of a discipline: there is no achievement if there is no challenge. But what is challenged in art is feeling in terms of what Mr Pasmore calls "mental structure". The younger child can express a feeling spontaneously because feeling itself is spontaneous; but the adolescent (by reason of basically physical changes) becomes aware of feeling, and needs to define feeling in order to come to terms with life itself. Art is the definition of feeling, but somehow the feeling must be preserved. "I love the rule that corrects the emotion," said Braque, but added, "I love the emotion that corrects the rule."

'Art education itself is in its infancy. Perhaps it has now reached its adolescent stage. We have not solved the problem of teaching art to the adolescent, but one of the beneficial results of the *Sunday Pictorial* Exhibitions of Children's Art has been to focus attention at a national level on this insistent problem.'

R. R. Tomlinson

'The members of the selection committee have, throughout the years the exhibition has been presented, felt a sense of disappointment at the poor quality of the bulk of the work submitted by the older age groups as compared with the stimulating and refreshing work of the younger children. This is not surprising as it is recognized by authorities that at the onset of puberty the urge to create undergoes strain and in many cases ceases if the cause is not understood by sympathetic teachers. One of the early pioneer teachers of modern methods formed the opinion that, at this stage, the creative power of both boys and girls became dormant, in girls at a somewhat older age than in boys. Experience since that time has shown that this is not so, that it can, by skilful teaching, continue to develop and mature. Of the successful methods used to tide over this critical period of development, perhaps the most effective has been by the introduction of new materials, such as clay, and the practice of various crafts, particularly three dimensional, as the appreciation of an interest in form is aroused at this age. One of the most useful crafts for this purpose is puppetry and its plays, when words replace images, with its associated crafts, lighting and scene painting. The painting involved often renews the waning interest in painting. Other authorities advocate some formal teaching: objective drawing, the study of colour and its relation to form. They also encourage personal discovery through the study of nature. Through these means they enrich and develop the power to express creative ideas. The responsibility for bridging the gap between the innate means of expression of the child and the increasing awareness, at the age of puberty, of adult forms of expression and modern shapes and forms is that of the teacher.

'The art teacher should act as a go-between, helping the older boy or girl to see and feel some of the modern values as well as those of the past. The selection committee ventures to hope that the views they have expressed may prove of value to both teachers and parents alike in solving what they believe to be a matter of vital importance to the usefulness and development of art education in our schools.'

Andrew Nairn

'Certain elements in the work submitted each year appear to be constant and satisfactory, and these are mostly to be found in the two younger age groups, painting freely and uninhibitedly in the manner now generally expected from young children. Their drawings are direct in vision and uncomplicated in meaning, often lyrically decorative, frequently amusing, with the simple pleasure of manipulating the medium always apparent. This "child art" aspect has become an integral part of the National Exhibition, and is probably the one which has had the greatest appeal throughout the country, influencing teachers who had themselves been reared in the sterner academic tradition, and generally spreading a better knowledge of the child's point of view.

'Most of the doubts increasingly expressed by the Advisory Committee and its selectors have been concerning the older age groups, and particularly that of fourteen to sixteen, when the happy abandon of child art is not enough and yet no serious sense of direction or purpose has succeeded it. It has long been recognized that this point is the greatest difficulty the specialist art teacher has to meet. The form of teaching has been blamed for a stifling of creative urge, but it persists for those who are themselves the products of newer methods of study and training. It seems obvious that the many children are discarding the fairy story, while the few have not yet emerged into the stage of concentrated and intensive thought and effort which marks the serious art student, whom I should place around the age of eighteen rather than sixteen.

'It may be that during this period of imaginative recession and before the arrival of other standards, more satisfaction can be attained by stressing design and the crafts, with a specific task set, and certainly in many schools I find the potters, the screen-printers, the model-makers and the puppeteers showing a better grasp, than in the painting at that age. Here they often seem to produce their best effort in a higher degree of representation (which has never really been a characteristic of this exhibition), drawing the things they see with as much accuracy as they can, though with varying degree of personal interpretation—the figure, the industrial city or country scene, ships, trees, flowers or still life—concrete subject matter when the purely imaginative field has become vague and unrelated to their experience. There was abuse in the over-insistence on representational accuracy in the past, but this restriction always fell most heavily on the youngest children, now largely freed from it. Many people feel that the older secondary pupil and the art student still have need of a strong factual basis on which to build their work. However much it follows the mood of present-day adult painting (which is after all only one phase in a continuous development), I feel there is too much emphasis on the abstract or semi-abstract forms, which I do not think are often the natural means of expression of the boy or girl of fourteen or sixteen, and can become merely a new mannerism imposed by teaching to yet another formula. On the other hand, there are this year some notable examples of acute observation and technically accomplished recording which have a logic and conviction quite refreshing in their honesty, and are yet wholly individual in character.'

Gabriel White

'For the child, painting, drawing or a craft is the pleasure of creation and the satisfaction in discovering how hand and eye can co-operate and how materials can be controlled for a definite purpose. The images that result may spring from deep within and have a long history before they emerge from the child's mind or possibly may come from without, from the suggestions and example of the teacher, and there is limitation rather than creation. Occasionally we find a desire to depict the outside world; then a child enjoys the freedom of changing nature and even at times producing the monstrously unnatural. Often symbolization is its artistic language, which can result in astonishing poetic effects and not infrequently discloses a latent observation and even sense of character.

'The educative merit of art lies in the need it creates within the child to realize its environment and give shape to its fantasies so that they acquire a valid existence. Herein lay the criticism of earlier methods of teaching the arts to the very young. Discipline was instilled before a desire could develop to acquire this new faculty. One suspects the boredom of these early classes has been exaggerated, and even the bowler hat and watering can evoked just as strange images as we have now and gave satisfaction to their creator. The hard pencil and the barring of colour were not, however, conducive to much pleasure. We sometimes forget how easily the young can absorb new disciplines, which will later become irksome and difficult to master. The bridge from child to adolescent art has in recent years become the chief problem in art education at schools. The gay and pleasure-giving images of early childhood become dull and inhibited with the older age groups. The supporters of modern art education contend that the latter have never had a chance to carry on their work, and that the marked drop in achievement is due to insufficient opportunities and to the overwhelming competition of rival interests, whilst the critics of child art are ready to assume that there is an unsurpassable break between it and the teaching of older children which may, in turn, be the foundation for the education of those who wish to make art their profession.

'Wherever the truth may lie, the spontaneity of earlier work—and here lies its greatest charm—must, at some time, give way to self-consciousness and a desire to master these powers of image-making. The vocabulary must be enriched and the possibilities of the various media learnt. During this period we may have to accept a dullness, a lack of originality and a sense of effort, which makes these pictures poor competitors with what has gone before. In fact, what is deplored may be desirable and be a concealment of real achievement. All who teach art students know that the student who produces his best work at school is not necessarily the one who will produce the best in ten years' time.

'We can see the same phases of development with the adult Sunday painter, and unless the Sundays are few and far between, the freshness and originality of the first efforts cannot be repeated indefinitely. But even if we admit that we are perhaps expecting too much from the pictures of older children, there is still much to be done in developing the art education for the eleven-year-olds and onwards. It may be that we must accept as part of the process of growing up a period when the average child, especially boys, cannot be interested in the arts, and more harm than good is done to force him then rather than to wait a year or two, when later he will again be more receptive.'

E. M. O'R. Dickey

'Works of art speak for themselves to older girls and boys, who, in their turn, sometimes tell us what they really think of them. A boy praised Picasso for "a violent form of life inside of him". Another thought Henry Moore's reclining woman at the Tate should be placed outside—"a lazy figure lounging on the grass".

A girl, praising today's building compared with that of the eighteenth century, wrote, "The architect now does not concentrate on beauty but on geometrical shapes." Then there was the girl who found the famous Leonardo in the National Gallery "wonderfull" and "marvelouse" and described the subject as "the Virgin sitting on some rocks with some children"; the boy who thought Rembrandt's self-portraits were those of a "doddering old drunkard", and the girl who, seeing the Mona Lisa in the Louvre while in Paris on a school journey, thought it inferior to the reproductions she had seen at home. No art master told any of these teenagers what to think. They just reacted in their own way. Perhaps the science sixth tend to approach art from a matter-of-fact point of view which imposes a severe test on the artists, and perhaps the classical sixth are inclined to be more sympathetic, but all will be interested and the teacher knows that older boys and girls have a powerful response to works of art and that it is the individual's genuine reaction which counts: art master and head-master will do well to provide encouragement, opportunity and lots and lots of information.

'But, as we can see from our exhibition, the teenagers want to draw and paint and to make things as well as to look at them. Here it is more difficult for the older child to be satisfied with what he has done than for the youngster.

'Now the art master faces another challenge, and he will give those who "can't draw" some ready means of creative expression and at the same time he will be on his toes to respond to the needs of the gifted pupil. The winners of our scholarship can bear witness to the help they have received from their teachers—as indeed can the rest of the exhibitors.'

Eduardo Paolozzi

'What emerges clearly now from the examination of the several layers of expression, the works painted by the different age groups, is the constant magic and appeal described by the images of the youngest children. The muscular smears and urgent marks—dismembered traces and shaky dribbles bear a marked resemblance to specific types of modern abstract art. The motivations and drives of these two worlds could not be more dissimilar and yet the arrangement of forms, line and shape of these two forces attract similar responses.

'An intelligent study oscillating between these two poles of attraction would supply additional valuable material for the study of the creative act. Chapter headings—Translation of experience. Metamorphosis of the idea. Double-metamorphosis of destruction. The brain and the gesture. Specific marks and degrees of ambiguity.

'Bridging the gap would lead to greater understanding and supply thoughts and guides for intelligent direction of twentieth century art pedagogy.

'Imagination, the pattern of progress, technology and ethnography lie within the general diagram of fast-moving cultural changes.

'Art as an activity, not distortion of the classical ideal. An activity spiritual and dynamic in sympathy with modern conditioning and scientific development.'

Victor Pasmore

'The new spirit in art teaching for children, following in the wake of modern developments in adult art, presents itself inevitably as a counterpart to the methods of classical education. Classical education was based on the principle of copy and imitation of the adult through the medium of established example. Drawing and painting were taught in the same way as Latin and arithmetic with the result that facility in imitation became the first requisite of child art practice.

'The revolution implicit in the new art teaching is that the child is not required to imitate the adult, but is asked instead to produce his own art. This means that the limitations of the child are accepted as an inevitable characteristic of his art. The process of teaching, therefore, is not one of correction according to example, but of encouragement towards natural development. Given the stimulus and the tools, the child teaches himself through the process of his own activity.

'The success of this approach with small children is now self evident. Nevertheless, one fact which emerges clearly and conclusively from the successive *Sunday Pictorial* exhibitions of modern child art is the extraordinary decline in the quality of work when it comes to the older children. Only one conclusion can be drawn from this; namely that, unlike the child, the new education has been unable to develop.

'The adolescent is at once self-conscious of his approaching maturity. On his own initiative he looks to the adult and despises the child. The term "child art", therefore, in its primitive form, cannot be applied to the adolescent. Nevertheless it is evident from the unsatisfactory response of the adolescent to the new art teaching, that the imagery and technical limitations of the small child are being imposed on all children irrespective of their age and development. Two unfortunate developments arise from this error: (i) both teacher and adolescent pupil tend to mistake sloppiness for freedom of expression and (ii) those teachers who realize something is wrong tend to abandon the new teaching directly the child reaches adolescence and revert to the old, imitative approach. Whereas the former represents a travesty of the principles of the new teaching, the latter is a negative reaction to the problem, depriving the adolescent of the benefits of his earlier teaching.

'But, just as the problem of adolescent art teaching cannot be solved by preventing the pupil's development, so it cannot be solved by reaction. In reality what is required of the adolescent in art is precisely the same, in principle, as that of the small child; namely, that he produces his own art. Allowances, however, must be made for development particularly in the mental,

rational and technical sphere. Mental structure and technical skill are essential factors in adolescent development; so that, unless adequate provision is made for these factors, the adolescent cannot be expected to take an interest in the new art teaching.'

Again, referring to the difficulties experienced by the upper age group, Frank Tuckett wrote, in his foreword to the 1963 catalogue:

'In the world in which we live today, children of all ages are subjected to the impact of countless images seen in books, on hoardings, and, not least of all, on the television and cinema screens. This impact is less in the case of the younger, unsophisticated child, as is confirmed and reflected by their ability to continue to produce quite naturally and spontaneously their innocent yet powerful statements, stemming from their own private world or from the world around them.

'On the other hand, it is not surprising to find that many of the older children are visually and mentally bewildered as they become conscious of a developing awareness of the diversity and complexity imposed on them by their environment. The more thoughtful the adolescent, the more bewildered he is likely to become as he struggles vainly to come to terms with it. The glut of visual material by which he is surrounded becomes a mixed blessing when mature judgments cannot yet be employed. Yet all around him for the finding is the challenge of exciting visual experiment of new materials and shapes and the wonder of unknown worlds opened up for his delight by the magic of the microscopic or macrocosmic view. Truly he lives in an exciting, stimulating and challenging time, a time when he might be expected to have more to say than ever before, with a larger potential vocabulary at his disposal with which to make his personal statement.'

Conclusions and Future Developments

We have seen that philosophers as far back as Aristotle and Plato realized the importance of training the hand as a means of developing the mind and the need for aesthetics in all forms of education. However, it was not until the eighteenth century that their reasoning was explored deeply enough to bring the significance of their principles to maturity.

Frustration from childhood through to adolescence and finally to manhood can be one of the greatest obstacles to true education and development. The need of the young child to express himself is paramount. If this desire, which is a perfectly natural one, is unnecessarily or unreasonably thwarted, the child quickly adopts aggressive or protective shields that spring from this frustration. The teacher should be able to appreciate the creative urge in the child, and to recognize the needs and stages of the child's development. The relationship of teacher and pupil should be one that will encourage the flowering of the child's imagination. It should be based on an understanding of the child's outlook and must primarily be a friendship rather than any form of dictatorship.

The art room provides a great opportunity to release and fulfil such desires. There the child can work with brushes, colours, lumps of clay and other materials to satisfy the creative instincts that are native to his being.

It is essential for the teacher to foster the enthusiasm of the children, and to accompany them in their explorations; then the way to self-expression is wide open. Each day can bring new ideas that may suggest fresh methods or reveal a new view of old techniques. Freshness and vigour should characterize the art room.

As a critic, the teacher treads on dangerous ground. A strong adverse opinion can at once stunt the flowering of the child's development. It can cause not only dismay but confusion of thought. To allow instruction to sink to the level of picking on small incorrect details is to dislodge the whole foundation of child art instruction. Enter the simple direct mind of the child and enjoy with it the moment when the vision appears on paper. What is there to look for? A natural rhythm, boldness, colour and fantasy. These are far more important in the early stages than accurate representation.

In the speed of growth of those early years insistence on neatness and detail can obstruct development. The child will begin to fear disapproval and will, often unconsciously, mould his work artificially in order to win praise. Again, to ask a child to explain in words what he is doing or has done is to risk making him feel that you do not understand. The mainstream of this self-expression is happiness; it does not need verbal explanation.

Writers like Herbart and Froebel fully realized the implications of this kind of creative education, and continually stressed the value of giving freedom to the imagination and creativeness of the child mind, underlining the importance of art and craft teaching as an integral part of general education.

Even so, art teaching was not introduced into state-aided schools until the middle of the nineteenth century. The early methods of teaching were for many years sterile, until the psychologists drew attention to the stages of development through which children pass, and the appropriate methods of teaching needed at each stage. Influenced by this knowledge, pioneer art teachers like

Ablett, Cizek and, latterly, Marion Richardson allowed children to express images in their own delightful way.

Mention has already been made of the beneficial effect upon art teaching made by new materials and by allowing children to see the work of others of their own age in exhibitions. There is, however, another outstanding development which deserves special mention, that is the realization of the importance of the right environment so that the hand, the eye and the imagination can work in unison. Training in looking and seeing should, therefore, supplement picture- and pattern-making and the various craft activities. This looking and seeing can become something that will enrich the lives of the children in the future. Many people live very narrow lives. Twice a day or more they may pass by some beautiful object, some subtlety of light or view, without observing them. Learning to look at these things can give almost another dimension in feeling, in living.

Sufficient credit has not been given to the vast improvements in the child's environments provided by the new modern school buildings and furnishings. Thirty or forty years ago most schoolrooms were dreary premises that spoke more of a penitentiary than of a place where enlightenment and enjoyment could come to the child. The classrooms were painted in dull, depressing colours, with mean desks on which mean materials were used. The content of the textbooks revealed an ignorance of the child's true interests. Today, happily, as fast as money can be made available, schools are being rebuilt. The new ones have become what they should be, places of light and warmth, comfortable and attractive. When the child can begin to enjoy his surroundings, the first step has been taken towards an undistorted view of school. Instead of being a burden, schooling starts to be an enjoyable progress.

Over the last century, particularly the last decade, changes made by enlightened architects and education authorities have been as revolutionary as any developments in methods of teaching. Comparisons between school buildings not yet replaced (some of them our public schools) and the new schools recently built in rural areas, reveal large windows, cheerful colour schemes and extensive playing fields. Special attention should be paid to the new comprehensive schools being built all over the country, and to their amenities and to the generous provision made in them for art and craft education.

In addition to encouraging children to make pictures and patterns and to practise various crafts, these activities should be supplemented by things of beauty and good design that are around them, like well-designed furniture, well-designed and well-printed fabrics, harmonious colour schemes. Perhaps the most formative innovation is the provision of pleasant and attractive colour schemes for the improvement of classroom atmosphere. Gone are the institutional browns, greys and greens; the new and exciting colour schemes are enriched by excellent colour reproductions of historic and contemporary paintings with specimens of fine craftsmanship and, if money is available or donors come forward, even by original works of art by local or well-known artists. Quite apart from the decorative value of these reproductions is the help they can give not only in the teaching of art history but of history in general. Pictures need to be changed regularly, and many educational authorities have formed circulating collections for this purpose. Although reproductions have their appropriate function, it is also important for children to have the opportunity not only to see but to live with original works of art. With this in mind, progressive authorities are forming their own collections of original works of art, painting, sculpture and specimens of well-designed objects of everyday use. The artists represented may range from world-famous masters to local painters or sculptors. Anything that can be done to stimulate imagination and thought is encouraged. Change can stimulate and spur the development.

Art is not static, but a lively and vital activity; it

must, therefore, either develop or decline. It has been said that to create is a natural instinct to be satisfied on the craft bench, the drawing boards and the easels in the classroom. The imagery in the mind of a child may be the embryo of a great picture or a fine design for the future. To see and enjoy as an artist, in one way or another, is the potential of all, but it is the way of realizing this vision that is the key to a future of greater fulfilment. Progressive teachers understand this need, and have made and are making useful experiments to find out how best to bridge the period from child art to man art. These researches have mainly been directed so far to those who wish to follow some branch of art as a profession, but soon their results will bring a true appreciation of art through understanding for everyone. Of particular interest are the methods used and experiments made at the Department of Fine Art, King's College, Durham University, Newcastle upon Tyne, at Leeds College of Art and Leicester College of Art. With these experiments and new methods of teaching are associated the names of Victor Pasmore, Harry Thubron, Eduardo Paolozzi and Tom Hudson. All four have acted on the selection panel for the National Exhibition of Children's Art.

Results of these new methods in the teaching of basic design and space and mass structures in both hand and machine techniques have been shown in recent exhibitions. Art authorities and teachers of art to children are satisfied that modern methods of teaching practised in schools today are right, particularly for young children, in spite of the fact that some eminent critics consider art education in primary and secondary schools a form of therapeutics through the imagination and doubt whether it has any effect on aesthetic appreciation in later life.

There is no doubt that in common with other absorbing activities, the practice of art by children has therapeutic value, but from the closer and extensive association with the teaching of art to children and the opportunity to follow school-leavers' careers that we have enjoyed, we are convinced that children who are allowed to exercise freely and develop their imaginations by picture-making and craft activity will live a fuller and richer life in whatever calling they may follow.

Children's Art from the Commonwealth

By happy chance, as this book was going to press, the Commonwealth Art Festival was held in London. Associated with it, exhibitions of art by children in Commonwealth countries were arranged in London and Cardiff. Both were organized by the *Sunday Mirror* and, with their kind permission, it has been possible to include illustrations of typical exhibits in this book. Some thirty-three countries submitted children's paintings and specimens of craftwork. Although the first choice was made in the countries that contributed, it was not possible to put on show the whole of the large amount of work received here. A selection committee under the chairmanship of Sir Herbert Read was, therefore, formed of the following members: Sir Robin Darwin, Principal of the Royal College of Art, where the London Exhibition was held, Miss Audrey Martin, Victor Pasmore and R. R. Tomlinson. This committee chose examples of paintings and craftwork most typical of the contributing countries. From this initial choice,

there was a further selection by the committee for exhibition in London, and a similar selection for showing in Cardiff made by Tom Hudson and Leslie Moore.

These exhibitions provided the opportunity to see the regional variations of the many contributing countries.

Drawing is a universal language and at first sight all children draw alike the world over, particularly when they are given suitable materials and conditions in which to work and are under the direction of understanding teachers. They are, however, inevitably influenced by national traditions and by their environment.

The exhibitions were much appreciated both in London and Cardiff, particularly by the large number of children and teachers who visited them. It is hoped that, in due course, we in this country will be given the opportunity to see children's work not only from Commonwealth countries but from countries the world over.

Paintings

1   A witch flying

Linden Allsop (6) *Morpeth County Infants' School, Northumberland*

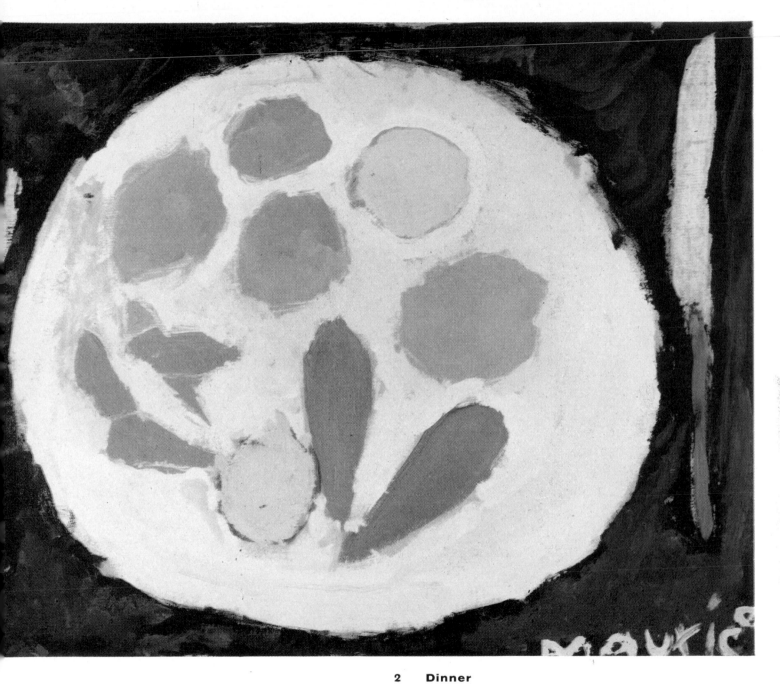

2   Dinner

Maurice Cliff (9) *Winterbourne Kingston Primary School, Dorset*

3   Mother showing baby the farm

Joan Newall (8) *Milton House School, Edinburgh*

4   The Irish fisherman

John Fearon (8) *Fonthill Junior School, Bristol*

5   A decorated horse

Ursula Berry (11) *Cleveland Avenue School, Darlington*

6   Visit to the zoo

Janet Brome (11) *Brockley Primary School, London SE4*

7   Selling pots

Sarah Brayshaw (9) *Winterbourne Kingston Primary School, Dorset*

8   Café scene

Douglas Boyd (16) *Walton-on-Thames, Surrey*

9   Two little girls playing by a tree

Bernadette Addison (5) *Gibbons Road Infants School, London, NW10*

10   Cat

Group work (12) *Hospital Secondary Modern School, Great Yarmouth*

11   What goes on in front of me?

Barry Lovell (10) *Brockley Primary School, London SE4*

12 The witch

Richard Nash (10) *Fonthill Junior School, Bristol*

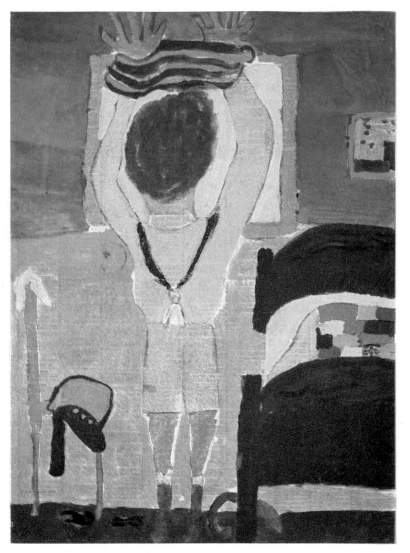

13 In the morning

Richard Walker (8) *Stratford Road Primary School, Birmingham*

14 Lady

Ruth Spain (10) *Residential School for Deaf Jewish Children, London SE12*

15   Guy Fawkes night

Elizabeth Ayres (6) *Bernards Heath Infants School, St Albans, Hertfordshire*

16 Muscle beach

John Creasor (16) *The College of Art, Middlesbrough*

17 Abstract

Diane Thubron (16) *The College of Art, Leeds*

18   Wasp on a flower

Ruth Lewis (12) *Eothen School, Caterham, Surrey*

19   Cat in the greenhouse

Ruth Cowan (11) *Godolphin and Latymer School, London W6*

20   A blossom tree

Peter Newsham (8) *Fonthill Junior School, Brist*

21   Waterfront

James Mellish (12) *George Abbot School for Boys, Guildford, Surrey*

22   **Teacher playing piano**

June Clevitt (7) *Cornhill Primary School, Aberdeen*

23 Hornsea church

Peter Jobling (12) *The Grammar School, Hull*

24　Autumn trees

Dinah Jones (17) *Townmead School, West Drayton, Middlesex*

25 Hyacinths

Rosemary Glover (7) *Dodsworth Road School, Barnsley*

26 Fish boxes

Eric Delf (15) *Saturday Morning Class, Lowestoft School of Art, Norfolk*

27   Drawing from my sketch book

Anne Vane-Wright (15) *Chislehurst and Sidcup County Technical School, Kent*

28 Harvesters

Shirley Bloomfield (16) *Eothen School, Caterham, Surrey*

29 Snow pasture

Jennifer Durie (14) *Redland High School, Bristol*

30 Portrait of Ann

John Brooke (16) *Epsom, Surrey*

31   People at work

Brian Baily (10) *Brockley Primary School, London SE4*

2   Irene Bell with a flower

Constance House (16) *Woolwich Polytechnic, London SE18*

3   Brenda Spragg

Margaret Duncan (14) *West Molesey County Secondary School, Surrey*

34   Painting no. 10

Peter Goddard (17) *Ilkeston, Derbyshire*

35   Riders

Terence Keating (14) *Wimbledon College, London SW 19*

36   Durham landscape

John Virtue (16) *Accrington, Lincolnshire*

37   Stern of a boat

Frank Dolphin (15) *Gravesend School of Art and Crafts, Kent*

38 Milking

Claudia Williams (15) *Eothen School, Caterham, Surrey*

39   Line rhythms

Colin Parker (12) *Alderman Cape Secondary Modern School, Crook, Co. Durham*

40   Road workers

Brian Cooper (16) *Plimsoll Road, London N4*

41 Flower drawing

Una Collins (15) *Chislehurst and Sidcup County Technical School, Kent*

42 Transport café, Moss Side

Peter Riley (16) *Oldham, Lancashire*

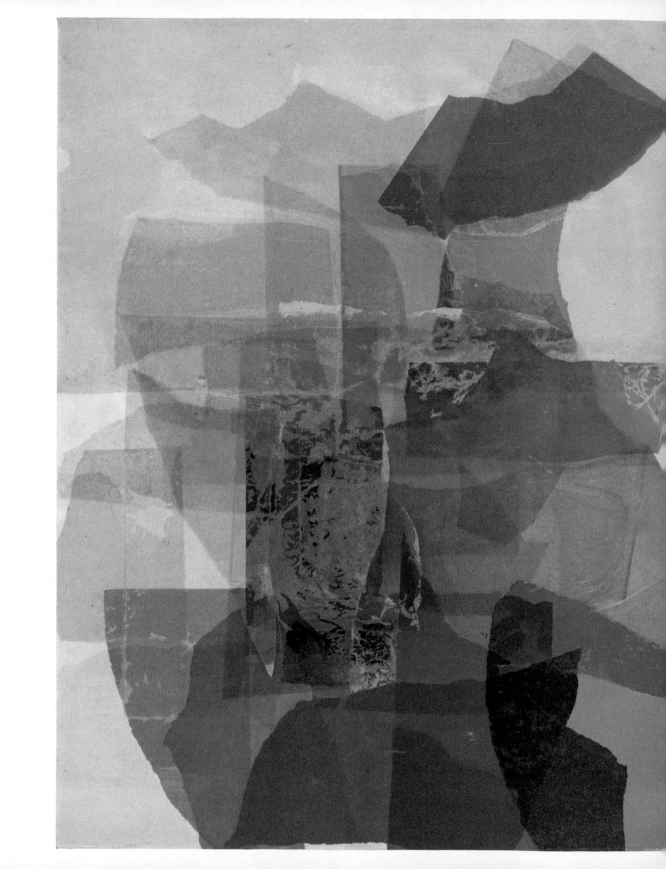

44 Le Seoube

Richard Napper (15) *Newcastle upon Tyne*

43 Composition in tissue

Susan Bradley (13) *Sidcot School, Winscombe, Somerset*

45   Red and black pattern

Heather Mackenzie *New Zealand*

46　A temple

Lam Mo-Yan *Hong Kong*

47   Man cultivating his orchard

Kyriakos Kyriakou *Cyprus*

48 Forest fire

Brian Teed *Canada*

49 Republic day

Parekh Amrit *India*

50   Grey houses

Chin Lai-Kwan *Hong Kong*

51 Cats

Ashutosh Mathur *India*

52 Wandering cat

Law Ching-Mei *Hong Kong*

53 Landscape

Sunalinie De Mel *Ceylon*

Drawings

FOSTER BY
B. CARTER 2C

54   Portrait of Foster

Brian Carter (13) *Cray Valley Technical School, Sidcup, Kent*

55   Hamid wearing his glasses

Diane Wright (8) *Plumcroft Primary School, London SE18*

56   Portrait of a friend

Barry Gibbs (11) *Cray Valley Technical School, Sidcup, Kent*

57   Bird shag

Eileen Allanson (13) *Victoria Street Secondary Modern Girls School, Middlesbrough*

58   Watching the birds

Valerie Norgate (14) *Danemark Schoo
Winchester, Hampshire*

59   M. Clipson

Philip Gebbett (14) *Cray Valley Technical School, Sidcup, Kent*

60   Yvonne, posing

Janet Kennett (12) *Halesowen County Modern Girls School, Birmingham*

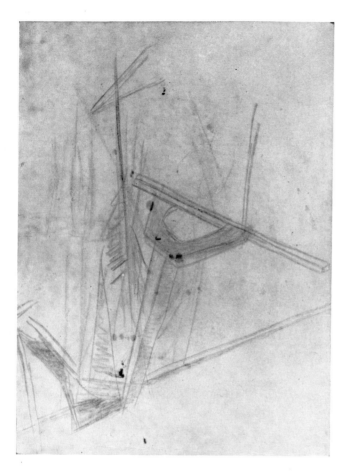

61   Charcoal drawing no. 2

Peter Goddard (17) *Ilkeston, Derbyshire*

62   Charcoal drawing no. 3

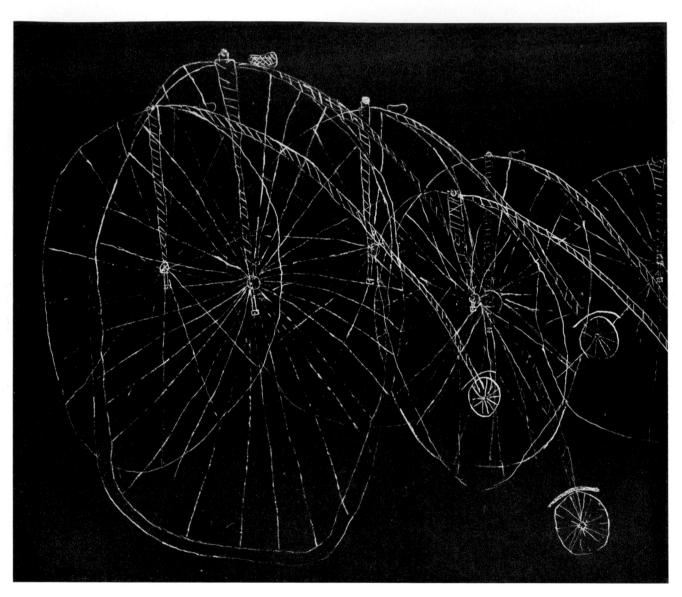

63 Penny farthing bikes

Stephen Phillips (12) *Mundella Secondary Modern School, Leicestershire*

64   Talking in the rain

Christopher Chardes (9) *Blackthorn County Primary School, Welwyn Garden City, Hertfordshire*

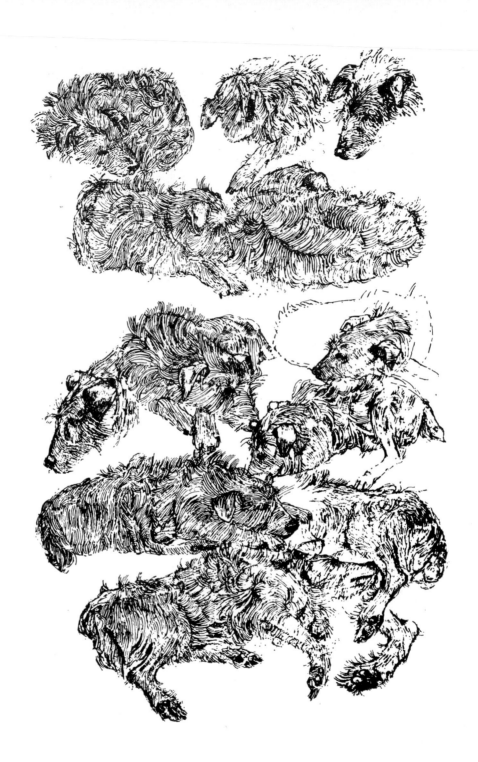

65-67 Sketches

Ralph Wardle (16) *Skellow, Doncaster*

68   Old lady no. 1

June Spencer (9) *Fonthill Junior School, Bristol*

Prints

69　Football match

Terry Dickel (11) *Ashburton County Secondary School, London E16*

70　Miners

Terry Richards (14) *Lescudjack Secondary Modern Boys School, Penzance, Cornwall*

71   Tired (etching)

Albert Mansfield (14) *Baguley Hall Secondary School, Manchester*

72 The thrush

Kenneth Wadcock (14) *Baguley Hall Secondary School, Manchester*

73   Kings and queens (Fabric print)

Group work (8 and 9)
Hallfield School, London W2

74   Industrial scene

Martin Wheeler (11) *Wyke County Junior School, Bradford, Yorkshire*

75   Dream city

Gregory Drabwell (16) *Harrow School of Art, Middlesex*

76   Printed fabric

David Nimmo (15) *Woolwich Polytechnic, London SE18*

77   Lino cut

Jenifer Brown (15) *Clifton High School, Bristol*

Crafts

78　The bull

Geoffrey Shepherd (17) *Grimsby Wintringham Boys Grammar School, Lincolnshire*

79   A cruel witch

Janet Downes (7) *Grove Infants School, Rayleigh, Essex*

80   Bird scarer

Susan Chambers (7) *West Heath Infants School, Birmingham*

81 Acrobats (clay)

Group work (11) *Burnt Mill Comprehensive School, Harlow, Essex*

82   Owl mask (papier mâché)

Robert Seddon (7) *Barnfield Primary School, Edgware, Middlesex*

83   Coronation piece (plaster)

Stephen Sillett and Colin Wood (14) *The George Mitchell School, London E10*

84 **Pig no. 2 (glazed terracotta)**

Paul Kenny (10) *Manchester Residential Open Air School, Styal, Cheshire*

85   Philippa my cousin on Prince (fired clay)

Elizabeth Needham (10) *St Stephen's School, Lansdown, Bath*

86 Refugee heads (plaster)

Robert Worsley and Derek Smith (13) *Howard School, Welwyn Garden City, Hertfordshire*

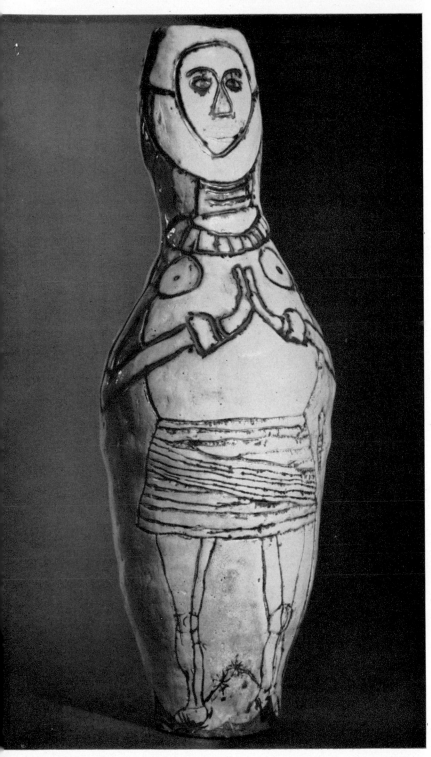

87 Brass rubbing (terracotta pot)

Edward Jenner (13) *Crown Woods School, London SE9*

88   Mounted knight (appliquéd felt)

Janet Warrilow (14) *Firrhill Secondary School, Edinburgh*

89 St Francis of Assisi (embroidered panel)

Group work (13) *Bebington Girls School, Cheshire*

90　Tiger (papier mâché)

Nicholas Munson (10) *Tollesbury County Primary School, Maldon, Essex*

91　Imaginary animal

Marion Morley (12) *Sherwood Hall Girls School, Mansfield, Nottinghamshire*

92 Cyclist
Anthony Short (15) *Ilford County High School for Boys, Essex*

93 Head of warrior
Brian Grote (15) *The Lennard School, South Ockenden, Essex*

94   Mexican Pete (terracotta)

Fergus McClelland (10) *Hallfield Junior School, London W2*

96   Felix the cat (terracotta)

Brian Shepherd (14) *North Romford Comprehensive School, Essex*

95   Tile bird (terracotta)

Mary Riordan (12) *Cardinal Manning School, London W10*

97   Fairy palace (wood)

Julian Young (7) *Spring Bank Infants School, Leeds*

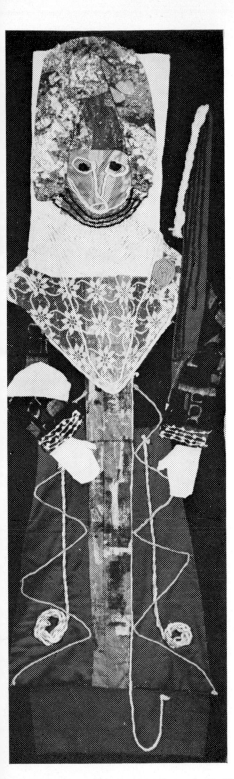

99 David (cloth doll)

Suzanne Rawsthorne (6)
Ralph Butterfield County Primary School, Yorkshire

98 Queen (lace, wool and cloth)

Sandra Preston and Rosanna Widowson (13) *Lucton Girls School, Loughton, Essex*

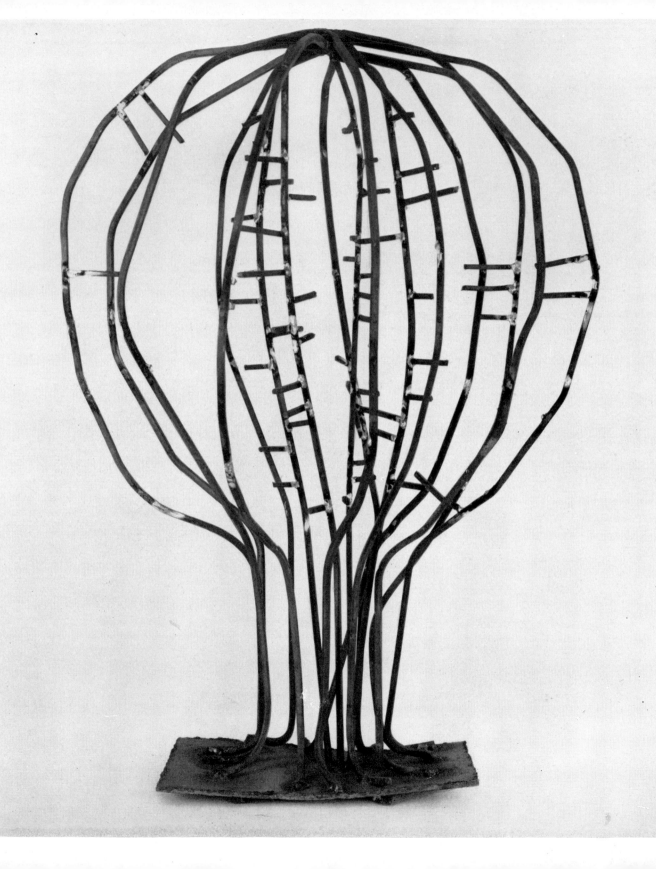

101 The Twelve Apostles (clay and wood)
Group work (12 to 14) *Lady Margaret School, London SW6*

Carnivorous plant (iron)
Howard Fry (16) *The College of Art, Leeds*

102 Fred (metal)

Group work (14) *Gateacre School, Liverpool*

103 Small coiled pot

Olamide Peters *Nigeria*

104 Coiled triangular pot

Ikwo Ekpoage *Nigeria*

105 Squaw and papoose

L. Manasco *Gibraltar*

106 Aboriginal hand tool

Australia

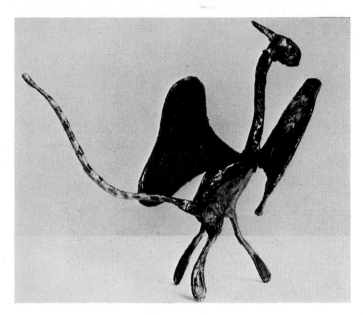

107 Imaginary animal
Warren Stringer *New Zealand*

108 Imaginary animal
Grant Smith *New Zealand*

Acknowledgments

We should like to thank the SUNDAY MIRROR for the help they have given in the preparation of this book, for the loan of the blocks, and for permission to quote from the catalogues of the National Exhibitions of Children's Art.

We also wish to express our appreciation of the assistance so generously given by Dr Alec Hay, formerly Chief Inspector of Education to the London County Council, who patiently read the manuscript and gave advice upon the text.

R. R. Tomlinson and John FitzMaurice Mills

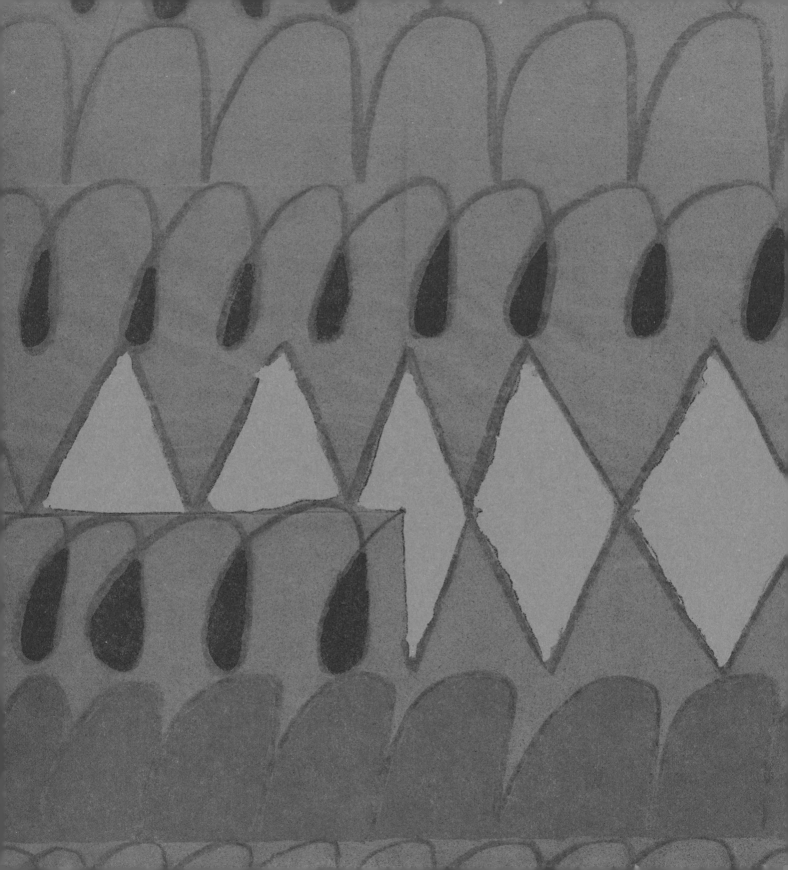